THE BIRDMAN

VERONIKA MARTENOVA CHARLES

Illustrated by

ANNOUCHKA GRAVEL GALOUCHKO & STÉPHAN DAIGLE

TUNDRA BOOKS

Published in Canada by Tundra Books,
75 Sherbourne Street, Toronto, Ontario M5A 2P9

Published in the United States by Tundra Books of Northern New York,
P.O. Box 1030, Plattsburgh, New York 12901

Library of Congress Control Number: 2005910622

Library and Archives Canada Cataloguing in Publication

Charles, Veronika Martenova
 The birdman / Veronika Martenova Charles ; illustrated by
Annouchka Gravel Galouchko and Stéphan Daigle.

ISBN-13: 978-0-88776-740-1
ISBN-10: 0-88776-740-0

 1. Noor Nobi — Juvenile fiction. 2. Wild bird trade — Juvenile fiction.
3. Calcutta (India) — Juvenile fiction. I. Gravel Galouchko, Annouchka, 1960-
II. Daigle, Stéphan III. Title.

PS8555.H42242B57 2006   jC813'.54   C2005-907312-8

We acknowledge the financial support of the Government of Canada through the
Book Publishing Industry Development Program (BPIDP) and that of the Government
of Ontario through the Ontario Media Development Corporation's Ontario Book
Initiative. We further acknowledge the support of the Canada Council for the Arts and
the Ontario Arts Council for our publishing program.

ONTARIO ARTS COUNCIL
CONSEIL DES ARTS DE L'ONTARIO

The illustrations for this book were rendered in gouache on Arches paper

Design: Kong Njo

Printed and bound in China

1 2 3 4 5 6   11 10 09 08 07 06

For Noor Nobi

– V. M.C.

To the knowledge of the heart

– A.G.G. & S.D.

Noor Nobi lived in the big bustling city of Calcutta. In the little laneways among the crumbling houses, the air hung heavy with heat and hummed with the sound of sewing machines.

The sun-scorched ground was littered with mango pits, melon rinds, black banana peels – and with scraps of colorful fabric and thread.

Many tailors worked there. Just like his father and grandfather, Noor Nobi labored every day, sewing baby clothes.

First he pulled a piece of fabric from the stack. He carefully measured it, marked it with chalk, and cut it to the size of a brown paper pattern. Then he sewed a tiny dress with neat rows of stitches, adding a collar and ribbons and ruffles.

Sometimes while he sewed, birds waited for bits of thread. Noor Nobi made sure to drop a few scraps now and then so they could weave them into their nests. Noor Nobi enjoyed his work, but more than anything, he loved his three children.

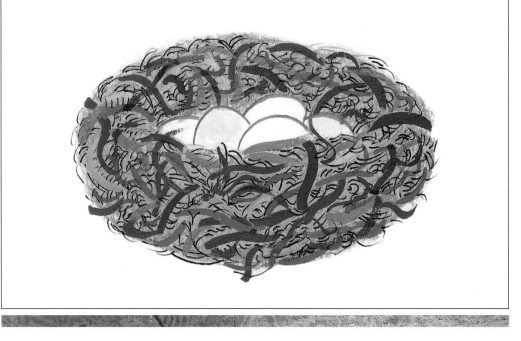

Seven days a week, from dawn to dusk, Noor Nobi worked to feed his little ones and to keep a roof over their heads. He was working when the accident happened – the accident that took them from him forever.

For many weeks after that, the sewing machine stood silent. Even the birds stayed away. Noor Nobi was overwhelmed with grief. He sat alone, staring at the walls, unable even to cry. Just as the rain refused to relieve the parched earth, no tears would come to wash away Noor Nobi's despair.

Then one day, Noor Nobi went outside.

The thick heat wrapped itself around him, but he didn't feel it. He wandered aimlessly through the hot, thirsty city.

The road was filled with cars, buses, wheelbarrows, animals, and rickshaws, all trying to avoid each other. There was honking and squealing everywhere, but Noor Nobi was blind and deaf to it.

Hours later, Noor Nobi found himself in a large market. Nothing – not the tables heaped with fruits, vegetables, and spices, not the pots and clothes that hung everywhere – caught his eye. But when he came to cages and cages crammed with birds, Noor Nobi saw those.

Poor creatures! Once they were free and now they are miserable, he thought. *Life is so precious and fragile. In an instant it can change or be snatched away.* For the first time in days, Noor Nobi allowed himself to think of his children.

"No magic can bring my little ones back,"
Noor Nobi admitted, "but maybe I can help
these small creatures and relieve them of their pain."
Noor Nobi reached deep into his pocket and found
almost nothing there.

He watched as people bought the birds and carried
them away. Finally, only one remained. "How much
for that bird?" Noor Nobi asked the vendor.

"Whatever you can pay,"
the man replied.
"I'm closing now."

Noor Nobi bought
the bird and carried it
through the dusty laneways,
past the houses, until he
came to an open space.

There, in the shade of a big banyan tree, Noor Nobi took the bird out of its cage. The trembling creature spread its wings and fluttered into the air.

Noor Nobi watched the bird fly to its freedom and thought of his children. This time, the emptiness in his heart filled a bit.

"Next week, I'll buy more birds," Noor Nobi decided. He returned to his machine and sewed dresses late into the night. For six more days, he worked harder than he had ever worked before.

On Monday morning, the coins, heavy in Noor Nobi's pocket, jingled as he walked to the market.

Noor Nobi waited in the sweltering heat until noon, when the prices of unsold birds dropped. Only the small, sickly ones were left. This time, he bargained for as many birds as he could buy.

At home, he poured water into a bowl and sprinkled grain for the birds to eat. He nursed them back to health, and when they were well and strong, he took them to the big banyan tree.

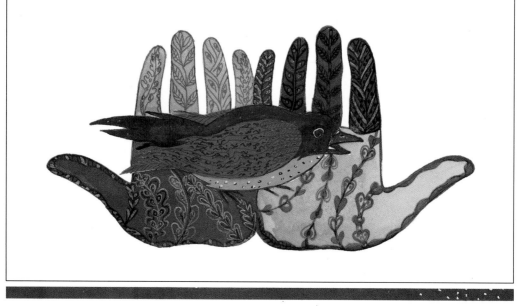

One at a time, Noor Nobi scooped them up and caressed their feathers. "Fly, Little One!" he whispered, as he released each bird in turn.

Timidly at first, the birds flapped their wings. Then they rose through the branches toward the open sky. Noor Nobi's heart soared with them.

As he watched, a few drops of water trickled down his face. Soon more poured down upon him. As Noor Nobi wept, the scorched, dry earth finally got relief. The monsoon rains had begun.

Noor Nobi is still a tailor for six days a week. But every seventh day – on Mondays – he is someone quite remarkable. On Mondays, Noor Nobi is the Birdman.

People come each week to watch what happens under the banyan tree. Some smile behind their hands, some say the Birdman is crazy, some stand respectfully, some think nothing at all. But most forget their troubles, just for a moment, each time a bird takes flight.

Today, the hum of sewing machines in the little laneways has been joined by the songs of thousands of freed birds.

And each week their songs grow louder.

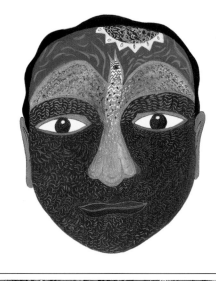

Noor Nobi

On a dreary November day not so long ago, an article appeared in *The Toronto Star*. The headline read "The 'Birdman of Calcutta' frees his flock." The story told of a man who had made it his mission – one rooted in personal tragedy – to free countless illegally caged birds.

Perhaps it was because I have a fascination with bird imagery. Perhaps it was because the man was a tailor, and I had spent many childhood hours playing games with buttons and fabric scraps beside my mother's sewing machine. Whatever the reason, I couldn't get the article out of my mind. I had to know more about this "Birdman." I called the newspaper and asked if they could put me in touch with the journalist who had written the story. The next morning my telephone rang.

Noor Nobi in his shop

"This is Azizur Rahman," said a voice over a crackling telephone line. "I'm calling from India. If you want to meet the Birdman, visit Calcutta and I'll introduce you to him myself. But if you are coming, you should do it before the monsoon season starts." I knew right then that if I didn't go, I would always regret it.

Noor Nobi choosing fabric

As I landed in Calcutta after twenty-six long hours of travel, I was not the only one wondering what on earth I was doing. Azizur was waiting for me with a shy and bewildered Birdman.

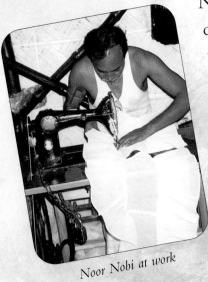

Noor Nobi at work

Noor Nobi – his real name – couldn't fathom why someone would come halfway around the world to meet him. I talked to him while Azizur translated, but it would take several days before I would come to know the real Noor Nobi, a proud, gentle man with a noble air about him.

During my stay I met Noor Nobi's new family and had many wonderful experiences. But the highlight of it all was my visit to his workshop.

Noor Nobi's second family

Azizur Rahman had driven me to the outskirts of the city – through crowds, past shacks and stalls – to the place where Noor Nobi works and lives. I became aware of a strange, yet familiar sound. "What's that?" I asked.

"There are some ten thousand sewing machines at work here," answered Azizur. "That is the song they sing."

Noor Nobi's daughter and her friends

Calcutta tailors

I peeked inside the doorways lining the narrow streets. Everywhere, in tiny closet-like rooms, men were bent over

Noor Nobi's work on display

humming machines. I could not find Noor Nobi, but as time passed, I became aware of a gathering crowd. They were waiting, just like I was, for something very special to happen. Eventually Noor Nobi came, carrying cages of birds he had purchased with his earnings. We watched as, one by one, he set the birds free in a ritual that was at once intimate, peaceful, and beautiful. It was then that I knew exactly why I had come.

Outside of Noor Nobi's shop

DIARY ENTRY

Calcutta, March 7

I'm sitting on the ground surrounded by scraps of fabric in Noor Nobi's workshop. As I did long ago I'm listening to the hum of a foot-driven sewing machine. Only this time I am not making up stories and acting them out as I did when I was a little girl. This time I am inside of the story itself. I am part of it... the story of a gentle man who is trying to make a small difference in the world) by saving the birds.

TO FLY: Noor Nobi Mollah feeds a bird rescued from a Calcutta market as he prepares to set it
The tailor spends up to a quarter of his income releasing illegally captured birds.

The Toronto Star article that began my journey

Prague, long ago, I am 4 years old, sitting with my mother by her sewing machine.